I0083345

The Promises of Jesus

A 31 Day Intensive Faith Therapy Devotional

By
Vanessa Collins

With Introduction by
Arlene Bell

Heart Thoughts Publishing
Floyds Knobs, IN

HEART THOUGHTS PUBLISHING

The Promises of Jesus
Copyright © 2012 by Vanessa Collins

Request for information should be addressed to:
Heart Thoughts Publishing, P.O. Box 536, Floyds Knobs, IN 47119

ISBN-13: 978-0-9823325-1-1
ISBN-10: 0-9823325-1-3
LCCN: 2012907129

Unless otherwise indicated, the Scriptures quoted are taken from the Authorized King James Version of the Bible. Other translations used - New King James Version (NKJV).

All rights reserved. This book or any portion thereof may not be reproduced or used in any manner whatsoever without the express written permission of the publisher except for the use of brief quotations in a book review.

Cover Design: Vanessa Collins
Editor: Janice McCauly

Printed in the United States of America

First Printing, 2012

Dedication

To Jesus, my Lord and Savior, my big brother: thank you for your promises.

To my wonderful husband Derrick and our wonderful children, Stephanie, Derrick II, David, and Tyrone and to my mom, Jean Crosby: thank you, again, for all that you do.

This book is especially dedicated to the 7 AM conference call family. Words cannot describe how much you have helped me over the last few years. Without you, this project would not have been conceived.

To my Pastor, Apostle Paul A. Southerland, the ultimate visionary, thank you for your obedience to the prophetic flow of the Holy Spirit.

To Judith Catlin, Mother Mary Hillmon, Mother Viree Curry, Yvonne Howell and Ron Jolla, words cannot describe how much you are missed.

Table of Contents

Introduction

And the Word was made flesh, and dwelt among us, (and we beheld his glory, the glory as of the only begotten of the Father,) full of grace and truth.

John 1:14

The book of John opens by telling us that Jesus Christ was the Word of God made flesh. What a profound statement, one that came with disbelief and confusion for some. How was that possible? What? Where did He get that from?

The writer of this book will take you on a fact finding mission and equip you with the tools necessary to believe without reservation. Until you do, consider this. During Jesus' time on earth (when the Word was made flesh, He proclaimed many things that pertain to you and me, even today. First, Jesus proclaimed the Kingdom of God and 2nd that the promises He left will lead all who believe to a victorious life in the kingdom.

If you are struggling with what you believe, at the end of this series you will KNOW what you believe and who you believe in by what the Word says. Get ready as you pray, study and meditate for the next 31 days. You will emerge a winner. Perhaps some of you may realize that you have already been equipped to be victorious in all areas of your life but not experiencing what you need.

Renew your mind to the Word of God and know that He is well able to fulfill any promises given...so receive, receive, receive...AMEN.

Arlene Bell

Day 1- Nothing Shall Hurt You

Scripture Lesson: Luke 10:19

> *Behold, I give you the authority to trample on serpents and scorpions, and over all the power of the enemy, and nothing shall by any means hurt you. (NKJV)*

Meditation

Today we are focusing on the promise that nothing shall hurt you. What an awesome promise. Most of us have had experiences in our lives that have hurt us. Many times we have blamed these experiences on the devil, our enemy. However, according to this scripture nothing is suppose to hurt us.

In this passage, the 70 disciples Jesus sent out had just returned. These were not the original 12. He sent them out in Luke chapter 9 with similar results. These 70 were "others" that were sent out by Jesus. They were full of joy and excitement as they exercised the power of Jesus on their own just as the 12 had done in the previous chapter. Jesus was not with them so they were excited to share with Him their experiences. Apparently, what really stood out for them was that "even the devils are subject unto us" through the name of Jesus. Jesus' response is our promise for today. He said that He has given us authority or power over serpents, scorpions and over all the power of the enemy and that nothing shall hurt us.

Are you dealing with hurtful experiences in your life? We have been taught that sometimes things will come to hurt us and that we have to "buck up" and learn how to handle the pain. We have to suffer with dignity and put a smile on our face. That all sounds well and good, however, it does not line up with this promise.

Jesus has given us authority or power over ALL of the power of the enemy. This is not speaking of who has more power. This says that you have authority over his power. You can tell the enemy what to do and where to go. You do not have to allow the enemy to run rampant in your life. Stop him in his tracks through the power of Jesus. How do we do this? Verse 17 tells us that it is through the name of Jesus. But be aware, the name of Jesus is not a simple, verbal stamp that you place at the end of a prayer. It is a strong belief in the power of Jesus Christ. Without that belief, you will find yourself like the sons of Sceva, in Act 19:13-16. They tried to use the name without the power, but were overcome. You have power. Believe it.

Affirmations

Jesus has given me the authority to trample on serpents and scorpions, and over all the power of the enemy. I rejoice and I am grateful for the promise that nothing shall by any means hurt me. I will no longer allow the enemy to exercise his power over me when Jesus has given me power over his power. I chose to shut the enemy down in my life today. In Jesus' name, Amen.

Day 2 - Abundant Life

Scripture Lesson: John 10:10

> *The thief cometh not, but for to steal, and to kill, and to destroy: I am come that they might have life, and that they might have it more abundantly.*

Meditation

Jesus not only came to give us eternal life, He came to give us abundant life. Eternal life speaks of our life in Christ after this experience of living is over. Abundant life speaks of this present life.

The dictionary tells us that the word abundant means "present in great quantity; more than adequate; over sufficient; well supplied; abounding, richly supplied". But what did it mean in Jesus' day? The word translated abundantly here is the Greek word *perissos*. According to the Strong's Dictionary of Greek words, *perissos* means 'exceeding some number or measure or rank or need, over and above, more than is necessary, superadded, exceeding abundantly, supremely, something further, more, much more than all, more plainly, superior, extraordinary, surpassing, uncommon, pre-eminence, superiority, advantage, more eminent, more remarkable, more excellent". It is clear that for many of us, we are living beneath our means.

Does this mean that Christians should have an abundance of material things? Or should we over spiritualize this scripture, as we do so many others, to say that Jesus was talking about an "abundant" spiritual life? Or does the truth lie somewhere in between? Our greatest clue comes from the beginning of this scripture. Jesus states that the thief comes to steal, kill and destroy. However, as a contrast, Jesus comes that we might have life and an abundant one at that. Can the thief steal, kill or destroy our spiritual life? He does not have that type of power. But he can steal our resources, kill our dreams and destroy our passion to work for the kingdom. While these may appear to be strictly "spiritual" things, they have many physical components. Kingdom work requires resources. And while we are to have an exceeding abundantly spiritual life, we can be of little help to the kingdom without proper resources. Jesus has, by grace, provided for that also.

Affirmations

Although the thief comes to kill, steal and destroy, I have learned that through Jesus I have been given authority over all of the power of the enemy. Therefore, I will accept the superior, exceeding, more remarkable, more excellent life that has been promised to me by Jesus. I rejoice and I am grateful for the promise of an abundant life. In Jesus' name, Amen.

Day 3 - All These Things Shall Be Added Unto You

Scripture Lesson: Matthew 6:33
>*But seek ye first the kingdom of God, and his righteousness; and all these things shall be added unto you.*

Meditation

In Matthew chapters 5-7, we find what many theologians have entitled "The Sermon on the Mount". In these series of teachings, Jesus covers a lot of ground including; the beatitudes, the Lord's Prayer, new laws, a proper attitude towards money and a host of other things. In chapter 6, we find His teaching on worry. It is out of this teaching that our promise for today is found.

Jesus instructs His listeners not to worry about anything, especially about things needed for their daily lives. We are not to worry about food, clothes, drink, nothing. There are several reasons that He gives for us not to worry. We should pay close attention to these.

1. God sees us as important. *Verse 26 - Behold the fowls of the air: for they sow not, neither do they reap, nor gather into barns; yet your heavenly Father feedeth them. Are ye not much better than they? Verse 30 - Wherefore, if God so clothe the grass of the field, which today is, and tomorrow is cast into the oven, shall he not much more clothe you, O ye of little faith?*

2. Worry does not produce anything. *Verse 27 - Which of you by taking thought can add one cubit unto his stature?*

3. Our Father knows that we have need of these things. *Verse 32 - (For after all these things do the Gentiles seek:) for your heavenly Father knoweth that ye have need of all these things.*

Many of us find ourselves worrying about our daily needs. It can be difficult to have a worry free attitude especially when we are faced with bills and obligations that seem to weigh us down. However, there is help for us. Our Father knows that we have need of these things; therefore we are commanded not to worry but to seek first God's Kingdom. But how do we do that? We trust God. We have faith in God. We obey God's Word.

Affirmations

I will not worry about my daily needs. I will first seek God's Kingdom. I will trust God. I will have faith in God. I will obey God's Word. I rejoice and I am grateful for the promise that, as I do this, everything that I need will be added to me. In Jesus' name, Amen.

Day 4 - All Things Are Possible

Scripture Lesson: Mark 9:23
Jesus said unto him, If thou canst believe, all things are possible to him that believeth.

Meditation

In a recent interview, Dr. Keith Black, who is an internationally renowned neurosurgeon and scientist, said the following,

"If you want to understand an artist, you study his art. If you want to understand God, you study nature because nature is the artwork of God. And there's nothing more incredible in the universe that I know of that I have ever imagined than the human brain."

The human brain is truly remarkable. It is the most complex machine we will ever operate however, most of us have no idea how it works. We know that it is located in our skulls and its functions include speech, thoughts and emotions. It is these higher functions of the human brain such as thoughts and emotions that make up what we understand to be the human mind.

We have also learned that much of what we have experienced, are experiencing and will experience in the future has a direct correlation to what we think and believe. If you were taught as a child that you were not important or you would not succeed, you probably experienced some negative things that were a direct result of those thoughts. Science has proven, beyond a shadow of a doubt, that a person's belief system has a major impact on that person's quality of life.

Well, before science made that remarkable discovery, Jesus explained it to a desperate father seeking help for his son. He had brought his son to Jesus' disciples, but they could not help him. Jesus gives this father a simple formula that seems too good to be true. Believe. If you can believe, all things are possible.

Here Jesus is, again, making those statements that we leaders in the Body of Christ must correct. Surely he didn't mean ALL THINGS are possible to him that believes. There must be limits. There must be "common sense" applied to these statements. Perhaps Jesus read the teleprompter wrong. He must get some better speech writers.

No, there was no error in what Jesus said, since He repeats this idea over and over again. And no, He did not read the teleprompter wrong. He meant what He said. What do you believe? What does the future look like for you? Do you believe that there is disaster at every turn? If so, you will surely find it. Or do you believe that God has a good plan for your life. If so, you will find it also. All things are possible (the good, the bad and the ugly) to him that believe.

Affirmations

I believe what the Word of God says. I believe that God has thoughts of peace, and not of evil towards me. I believe that by the stripes of Jesus I was healed. I believe that God will supply all of my needs according to His riches in glory. I believe that my steps are ordered by God. I rejoice and I am grateful for the promise that all things are possible to him that believe. In Jesus' name, Amen.

Day 5 - It Shall Be Done – The Law of Agreement

Scripture Lesson: Matthew 18:19

Again I say unto you, That if two of you shall agree on earth as touching any thing that they shall ask, it shall be done for them of my Father which is in heaven.

Meditation

Agreement on earth is a powerful thing. Nations have risen and fallen just on the power of agreement. The word "agree" means to concur or to consent to as a course of action. We have often misunderstood the word "touching" as used here to mean physical touch. The word translated here is "peri" which means about, concerning, on account of, because of, around, near. So we are told by Jesus in this scripture that if two people shall agree on earth concerning anything that they shall ask, it shall be done for them. What a powerful promise! Is God really prepared to back this up? We can come up with some pretty wild stuff. Does Jesus really know what He is saying?

Well, God has found himself in some very interesting positions because of this law of agreement. Now this law did not just come into effect when Jesus spoke about it. It has been in effect since God gave man freewill. And it as made for some very interesting times.

One of the most memorable is the Tower of Babel mentioned in Genesis 11. Although you may have heard differently, the Bible does not tell us that these people were wicked or that their motives were bad. We do know that their desire to build a city and a tower got God's attention and that He "came down" to see what they were doing. Since the word "heaven", used here, also means sky, God was not concerned that they would build a tower that would reach to where He abode. We have many skyscrapers today, so I do not think God has a problem with tall buildings. God seems to be concerned with the fact that these people, being on one accord, would be unlimited in what they could do.

So did God take their power away? Did He cancel the Law of Agreement? No. He scattered them by changing their language. Did He tell them that they were wrong? No. He did not send a prophetic message to them. He just caused them to move. Guess what? They got with people of their own language, and they moved to other areas and did exactly what they were going to do there. They built cities and towers all over the world. Perhaps it wasn't what they were agreeing to do that was the problem. It was who they were agreeing with.

Maybe you find yourself in the same place. God may be stirring things up not because of what you are believing Him for, but maybe it is who you are agreeing with. If the language people around you are using is becoming confusing, perhaps it is time to move on. Since we have been on this journey of renewing our minds, I am sure that our language has become confusing to many. We are not talking about lack and sickness and the works of the enemy. We are proclaiming the power of God in our lives.

Affirmations

I agree with the Word of God. I am who it says I am. I have what it says I have. I will seek God's wisdom when I agree with someone concerning their prayers. I rejoice and I am grateful for the promise that when we agree concerning anything, it will be done for us. In Jesus' name, Amen.

Day 6 - A Rewarder of Them That Seek Him

Scripture Lesson: Hebrews 11:6

But without faith it is impossible to please him: for he that cometh to God must believe that he is, and that he is a rewarder of them that diligently seek him.

Meditation

The writer of Hebrews opens this famous chapter with what has been called the basic definition of faith. It is a definition that many of us can repeat from memory. Faith is the substance of things hoped for, the evidence of things not seen. We are told in this chapter that it is by faith the worlds were framed through the Word of God. He then tells us about Abel and how it was by faith that his sacrifice was accepted.

The author then tells us about a little known person, Enoch. We are told here, and in Genesis 5:18-24, that Enoch was translated by God, meaning that he did not experience death. God just took him. We don't know much about Enoch from the traditional Bible. However, we are told in Heb 11:5 that Enoch pleased God.

The author pauses from his list of Old Testament saints to give us a sidebar, which is our scripture promise for today. We are told that without faith, it is impossible to please God. What a strange thing to please God with. You would think that obedience, sacrifice, prayer, or a host of others things would rank up before faith.

When you look at the list of heroes listed in Hebrews chapter 11, it becomes a little clearer. These men and women did not live perfect lives, but they did display extraordinary faith. It is this faith that caused them to receive honorable mention here.

How do we exercise pleasing faith? We are told that we must believe that God is and that He is a rewarder of them that diligently seek Him. Are you diligently seeking God? If you are, have faith that your efforts will be rewarded greatly.

Affirmations

I love God and I want to please Him. I know that I must have faith and believe that God is. I am diligently seeking God. I rejoice and I am grateful for the promise that He is a rewarder of them that diligently seek Him. In Jesus' name, Amen.

Day 7 - I Will Not Leave You Comfortless

Scripture Lesson: John 14:18
I will not leave you comfortless: I will come to you.

Meditation

The disciples had walked with Jesus for over 3 years. They had witnessed miracles unlike the world had ever seen before. People were healed, demons were casted out and even the dead were raised. Not only had they seen miraculous wonders, they had performed some of their own. When Jesus sent them out in Luke chapter 9, they returned with glowing reports of healings and how even demons were under their command. Many people followed them. They were probably getting use to this life. That is until Jesus pulled the rug out from under them.

He told them that He was leaving. Going where, they wondered. Of course He gave them a super deep theological explanation about prepared places and mansions and going to the Father but they didn't understand. Whereever this place was not familiar to them. They knew it was not in Jerusalem or Judea or even Samaria. It didn't sound like Rome. Where was He going? Why couldn't He just give them a straight answer? All they knew was that they had left everything they knew to follow this man and now He was talking about leaving. The anxiety was building. This was not a good day.

Jesus knew their hearts were troubled and they were afraid. His words of comfort to them are our promise for today. I will not leave you comfortless: I will come to you. Jesus had introduced a new concept to them, the Holy Spirit. He explained to them that He would never leave them even though they may not see Him. He promised them that the Holy Spirit would comfort them, teach them and bring His word back to them.

That same power and comfort of the Holy Spirit is available to us today. When we feel alone or troubled or afraid, the Holy Spirit is right there to comfort us, guide us and bring the word of God back to our remembrance. We are never alone.

Affirmations

The Holy Spirit is my comforter. He is my teacher and my guide. I am never alone, so I do not have to be afraid. I rejoice and I am grateful for the promise that Jesus will not leave me comfortless. He will come to me whenever I need Him. In Jesus' Name, Amen.

Day 8 - The Power of the Holy Spirit

Scripture Lesson: Acts 1:8

But ye shall receive power, after that the Holy Ghost is come upon you: and ye shall be witnesses unto me both in Jerusalem, and in all Judaea, and in Samaria, and unto the uttermost part of the earth.

Meditation

For Jesus' disciples, this had been a wild month and a half. Jesus had been arrested, crucified, and resurrected. Their emotions had gone from extreme sorrow to sheer joy. Now they were ready to see what was to happen next. Would this be the time that Jesus restored the kingdom to Israel? They had been under Roman rule for many years. They were ready for total freedom.

They did not get the answer from Jesus that they wanted. Jesus told them not to worry about that. They had bigger fish to fry. It was time for them to get to work. However, they did not have everything that they would need. They would still need power. That power would come from the Holy Spirit.

The Holy Spirit would not only comfort them, as Jesus explained in John chapter 14, the Holy Spirit would also give them power; the power to be a witness of Him. A witness is one who can give a firsthand account of something seen, heard, or experienced: one who furnishes evidence. They were called to furnish this amazing experience to world and to present it in such a way that it would be believable.

How well did they do? How powerful was the Holy Spirit in their lives? Through this power, a group of 120 people were able to establish a religion that has over 2.1 billion people worldwide today. That does not even include the billions and billions that have passed on.

That same power is available to us today. We have the power through the Holy Spirit to be a witness of Jesus Christ. Through our witness, we are impacting more people than we know. We are also impacting future generations. But what legacy are we leaving? What will future generations say about our representation of God?

Affirmations

I have the power of the Holy Spirit in my life. Through His power, I can have an awesome witness for Jesus Christ. I am mindful that people are watching me. I want to present a witness of Jesus Christ that is true to His Word. I rejoice and I am grateful for the promise that I have the power of the Holy Spirit. In Jesus' Name, Amen.

Day 9 - Ask, Seek, Knock (Part 1)

Scripture Lesson: Matthew 7:7-11

Ask, and it shall be given you; seek, and ye shall find; knock, and it shall be opened unto you: For every one that asketh receiveth; and he that seeketh findeth; and to him that knocketh it shall be opened. Or what man is there of you, whom if his son ask bread, will he give him a stone? Or if he ask a fish, will he give him a serpent? If ye then, being evil, know how to give good gifts unto your children, how much more shall your Father which is in heaven give good things to them that ask him?

Meditation

In Matthew chapters 5-7, we find what many theologians have entitled "The Sermon on the Mount". In these series of teachings, Jesus covers a lot of ground including the beatitudes, the Lord's Prayer, new laws, a proper attitude towards money and a host of other things. In chapter 7, we find our promise for today is found.

In this set of promises, we are told the exact nature of the promises in verses 7 & 8. In verses 9 through 11, we are given the logic behind the promises and why we can trust the promises. In this portion of scripture, we are encouraged to ask God for what we want. This may seem to be a simple task, but it is not. There are many different teachings on the subject of asking God for things. Some say that you should not ask God for things, especially material things. Others teach that God is like a Santa Claus that you should provide your list to on a regular basis. However, the teaching that Jesus presents here is simple: ask, seek and knock.

We are told that if we ask, it shall be given unto us. To ask is to make our request known to God. This is consistent with Philippians 4:6. Like the old saying goes, many of us have not because we have asked not. We have allowed fear and doubt to keep us from even obeying the command to ask.

We are also told to seek. When we seek something, we are looking for something with the desire of finding it. Just because something is not apparent does not mean that it is not there. However, like a hidden, precious treasure, we must diligently search.

Lastly, we are told to knock. This is the hard one for most of us. The idea of knocking means to engage, to deliver a sharp blow or push. Knocking can be hard work. However, it is in this hard work that the doors will be opened. But once the doors are open, we must make the effort to walk through.

Are there things you desire from God? Perhaps you are looking at physical well-being, or financial security or a host of other things. Follow the instructions given in these verses. First, don't be afraid to ask God for what you want. You think it is too big? I doubt it. Then seek out those things through the Word of God with the expectation of finding it. And finally, when you have arrived at the destination, don't be afraid to knock. Don't just tap on the door of your dreams; knock hard. And of course, once the door has been opened, don't be afraid to enter in.

Affirmations

I will not be afraid to obey the Word of God. I will ask God for what I want. I will seek out opportunities that are in line with my request. I will not be afraid to knock on the door once I find it. I rejoice and I am grateful for the promise that everyone that asks receives; that seeks finds and that doors are open to them that knock. In Jesus' Name, Amen.

Day 10 - Ask, Seek, Knock (Part 2)

Scripture Lesson: Matthew 7:7-11

Ask, and it shall be given you; seek, and ye shall find; knock, and it shall be opened unto you: For every one that asketh receiveth; and he that seeketh findeth; and to him that knocketh it shall be opened. Or what man is there of you, whom if his son ask bread, will he give him a stone? Or if he ask a fish, will he give him a serpent? If ye then, being evil, know how to give good gifts unto your children, how much more shall your Father which is in heaven give good things to them that ask him?

Meditation

Yesterday we looked at the nature of the three promises given in these scriptures. We are told to ask, seek and knock. We cannot be afraid to ask God for what we want. We then must seek out those things through the Word of God with the expectation of finding it. And finally, when we have arrived at the destination, we cannot be afraid to knock.

Today, we will talk about the logic behind the promises. How can God make these types of promises? Is He serious? What is the force behind these promises?

The force behind these promises is love. Not just any kind of love, but the love a caring father. Jesus poses several questions to those that are listening in order to convince them of the certainty of these promises. For Jesus, these promises are what we would call a "no brainer".

What man is there that would give his son a stone if he asked for bread? Bread is for nourishment. What nourishment would you get from a stone? Absolutely none. What kind of man would give his son a serpent if he asked for a fish? Fish is also nourishment. Not only would the son not be nourished by the serpent, he would be in danger of being injured. Jesus then tells them that if they, being evil, know how to give good gifts to their children, how much more shall the heavenly Father give good things to them that ask?

This scripture comes up against a lot of teaching that says God allows bad things to happen to us to teach us a lesson. Yes, God does discipline His children just like fathers discipline their sons. But most fathers would not give their children stones to eat and serpents to bite them as a form of punishment.

We are told in this scripture that our Father will give us good things if we ask. We have learned that God has provided those things for us by His grace. Therefore, we can ask in confidence if we believe the promises and walk in this truth.

Affirmations

I am a child of God. He is my heavenly Father. As my Father, he would not give me stones for bread or serpents for fish. I rejoice and I am grateful for the promise that He gives good things to them that ask Him. In Jesus' Name, Amen.

Day 11 - It Shall Be Given Unto You

Scripture Lesson: Luke 6:30-38

Give to every man that asketh of thee; and of him that taketh away thy goods ask them not again. And as ye would that men should do to you, do ye also to them likewise. For if ye love them which love you, what thank have ye? for sinners also love those that love them. And if ye do good to them which do good to you, what thank have ye? for sinners also do even the same. And if ye lend to them of whom ye hope to receive, what thank have ye? for sinners also lend to sinners, to receive as much again. But love ye your enemies, and do good, and lend, hoping for nothing again; and your reward shall be great, and ye shall be the children of the Highest: for he is kind unto the unthankful and to the evil. Be ye therefore merciful, as your Father also is merciful. Judge not, and ye shall not be judged: condemn not, and ye shall not be condemned: forgive, and ye shall be forgiven: Give, and it shall be given unto you; good measure, pressed down, and shaken together, and running over, shall men give into your bosom. For with the same measure that ye mete withal it shall be measured to you again.

Meditation

In Luke chapter 6, Jesus teaches about love for enemies and judging others. It is nestled in these scriptures that he also teaches about lending and giving. But it is not what you may expect.

Many of us have passed beggars on the street. Perhaps we have given to them a few times, but generally we will pass them by. We think that they may do something illegal with the money. Besides, we want to be good stewards over our finances and do not want to cast our pearls to swine. We work hard for our money, and if we give to someone or something, we want to make sure that it is for a good cause.

What about loaning money to people? We have been taught that it is not good business to loan to someone that probably cannot repaid the loan. Jesus teaching blows a hole in both of these ways of thinking. We are not only to give to those that ask, but we are to lend to those that can't pay. What kind of teaching is that?

It is the kind of teaching in which our promise for today is found. We are told that even sinners lend and give to those that they expect can repay them. But we are to be different. We are to give and not expect to receive anything back from them. We are told if we do, our reward will be great.

Where will this reward come from? What kind of reward will it be? We are simply told to give. If we give, it will be given unto us, good measured, pressed down, shaken together and running over. Where will it come from? It will come from others. People will give to you. How? It is how the universe is set up. It was designed by God to operate this way.

What a wonderful promise. When we give, we set things in motion in the universe for that good to come back to us multiplied. Well what about the people we are giving to? They don't deserve it. Exactly. Luke 6:36 tells us to be merciful just as our Father is merciful. We are not to judge or condemn, just give. And when we give, we have a promise that what we receive will be far greater than what we gave.

Affirmations

I am a giver. I am a lender and not a borrower. I will give and not expect anything from the person that I give to. I know that my reward is great. I rejoice and I am grateful for the promise that if I give, more will come back to me. In Jesus Name, Amen.

Day 12 - It Should Obey You

Scripture Lesson: Luke 17:5-6

> *And the apostles said unto the Lord, Increase our faith. And the Lord said, If ye had faith as a grain of mustard seed, ye might say unto this sycamine tree, Be thou plucked up by the root, and be thou planted in the sea; and it should obey you.*

Meditation

We will begin our series on promises of faith. These are promises in the Word of God that specifically deal with faith. Although most of them sound the same, we will look at each one separately. Hopefully the sheer fact that they are repeated will have an impact on us.

Our promise today begins with the disciples making a request of Jesus to increase their faith. What was it that had occurred that made them feel they needed more faith? Did a sick person show up that required healing? Maybe a demon needed to be cast out? Or better yet, maybe the dead needed to be raised? Why did the disciples feel that they needed more faith?

We see that the disciples did not have a problem with healing the sick. They were sent out in Luke chapter 9 and came back with glowing reports. That was not the problem. In fact, there was no immediate need at the time. It wasn't something that they needed to do right then that made them ask for more faith. It was a hypothetical situation that made them cry out for help.

The problem was forgiveness. Jesus told them that they would have to forgive. Even if the person kept doing what they were doing, as long as they said, "I repent" or basically "I'm sorry", the disciples had to forgive them, even if they did the same thing 7 times. Their answer to this was that they would need some help. They would need more faith.

Jesus did not tell them how to get more faith. More faith was not what they needed. They needed to learn how to use the faith they had. His answer to them is our promise for today. If you have faith as a grain of mustard seed, you can speak to whatever it is that is in your way, even a tree, and it shall obey you.

Whether you need to speak against your hard heart of unforgiveness, sickness in your body or bills on your table, you can expect results if you can believe this promise.

Affirmations

God has given me a measure of faith. I can activate my faith by using my words to move those things in my life that hinder me. I rejoice and I am grateful for the promise that if I have faith as a grain of mustard seed, I can speak to hindrances in my life, and they will obey me. In Jesus' Name, Amen.

Day 13 - You Shall Have What You Say

Scripture Lesson: Mark 11:22-24

And Jesus answering saith unto them, Have faith in God. For verily I say unto you, That whosoever shall say unto this mountain, Be thou removed, and be thou cast into the sea; and shall not doubt in his heart, but shall believe that those things which he saith shall come to pass; he shall have whatsoever he saith. Therefore I say unto you, What things soever ye desire, when ye pray, believe that ye receive them, and ye shall have them.

Meditation

This week we are continuing our series on promises of faith. These are promises in the Word of God that specifically deal with faith. As we said before most of them sound the same. However, we will look at each one separately. Hopefully the sheer fact that they are repeated will have an impact on us.

Mark 11:22-24 is a foundational scripture for those that are associated with the faith movement. It is in scriptures like these that we learn about our responsibility in faith. Although it sounds religiously correct to sit back, let go and let God do everything, we learn in these scriptures that this is not the case. We are told that faith without works is dead. But what works? Do we have to be kind to our neighbors, give to our local church congregation or feed the hungry?

While those are all good things to do, I want to bring your attention to a pattern that seems to be emerging from each of these scriptures. It appears that if we want to address our faith in a serious, intensive way, we must start with addressing our speech. We must realize the impact of what we say, even when we are joking.

Mark 11:23 gives what some have called the Law of Confession. Jesus states anyone can have what they say. There are some qualifications. It must be said without doubt and with belief. Let's quickly look at each of these. Jesus says that you cannot doubt in your heart. The word heart here is defined as the soul or mind, as it is the fountain and seat of the thoughts, passions and desires. The second part is that you must believe that the things you say come to pass. Not just when you want them to come to pass. You must be convinced of the power of your words.

Well, Jesus has done it again. He has once again managed to teach stuff that we ministers and leaders must correct. Surely he did not mean "whosoever". This is way too powerful for just anyone to operate. What about the "whatsoever"? Surely this only works for important, meaningful stuff. Right? Read your Bible. Jesus repeats this in several scriptures. If He said "whosoever" and "whatsoever", that is what He meant.

I want to challenge you this week to meditate on this promise. Read it over and over again until you are convinced that it works. Life has already taught us how not to walk in this promise. Ask the Holy Spirit to teach you how to walk in this promise. And don't concern yourself about the "whosoevers" and the "whatsoevers" that you don't want it to work for. Focus on God, through the Holy Spirit, making this Word real for you.

Affirmations

I have faith in God. I know that my words are powerful. I believe that those things which I say will come to pass. I will not allow doubts to overtake my heart. I rejoice and I am grateful for the promise that those things which I say come to pass. In Jesus' Name, Amen.

Day 14 - Answered Prayer

Scripture Lesson: Mark 11:22-24

And Jesus answering saith unto them, Have faith in God. For verily I say unto you, That whosoever shall say unto this mountain, Be thou removed, and be thou cast into the sea; and shall not doubt in his heart, but shall believe that those things which he saith shall come to pass; he shall have whatsoever he saith. Therefore I say unto you, What things soever ye desire, when ye pray, believe that ye receive them, and ye shall have them

Meditation

Today we will look at the second part of this scripture. If verse 23 is the Law of Confession, then verse 24 could be called the Law of Answered Prayer. After stating a remarkable and, for many, an unbelievable statement about the power of words, Jesus follows it up with this remarkable statement on prayer. Whatever you desire when you pray, believe that you receive them and you shall have them. What a fantastic statement. But is it really credible? How can Jesus guarantee prayers, especially of such a broad nature? "Whatsoever you desire" can cover a lot of stuff, especially for people like us that are still dealing with issues of greed, envy and selfishness. What is the key here?

It appears that the key is "belief". According to this scripture, if you pray and you believe that you will receive it, Jesus has already told you what the answer is. The answer is yes. Not only does He make this tremendous promise here, but He says the same thing in John 14:13, John 15:7, and John 15:16 and in about 10 other places.

What about James 4:2-3? James said that you lust and have not, you desire to have and cannot obtain, you have not because you ask not and even if you ask you receive not because you ask amiss that you may consume it upon your lust. What about that? We are told by Paul in 2 Timothy 3:16 that all scripture is given by the inspiration of God and is profitable for doctrine. So how do we reconcile what James has recorded here with the 10 to 15 scriptures that are recorded to have been spoken by Jesus?

As with all Bible study, you have to read scripture in context. Although we do not have time now to do an in depth look at these scriptures, I do not believe that there are any contradictions. If you read the entire 4th chapter of James, you will see that he is speaking of those that are fighting and killing to obtain a desire. The word "desire" used here is not the same word used in Mark 11:24. The Greek word translated here as "desire" actually means to burn with zeal, to be heated or to boil with envy, hatred, anger.

So, who are you? Are you the group of people James was talking to that is fighting and killing to get what you want? If so, trust me, you are having lust and jealousy issues because you don't believe in the power of your words. If you did, then you would know that no one has anything that you cannot obtain. You are jealous when you believe that they have it but you can't. Or are you part of the group of believers, sitting at the feet of Jesus in awe of His power and of the power that He has given you? If so, you can rest assure that His word is truth. When you pray, you can have what you ask for if you believe.

Affirmations

I believe in the power of prayer. I know that my words are powerful. I believe that those things which I say will come to pass. I rejoice and I am grateful for the promise that whatsoever I pray for, believing, I shall receive. In Jesus' Name, Amen.

Day 15 - A Prepared Place

Scripture Lesson: John 14:1-3

Let not your heart be troubled: ye believe in God, believe also in me. In my Father's house are many mansions: if it were not so, I would have told you. I go to prepare a place for you. And if I go and prepare a place for you, I will come again, and receive you unto myself; that where I am, there ye may be also.

Meditation

It was a strange day the disciples probably thought. It was just all kind of strange. Jesus was acting strange, Judas was acting real strange and now it just all seemed, well, strange. First Jesus washed their feet at dinner, then Judas abruptly leaves and now Jesus was talking about leaving, again. He had mentioned this leaving thing before, but this time it was different. It seemed more imminent now.

Moving and travelling was something that the disciples were used to. For the last 3½ years, they had been on the move. But now Jesus was talking about going somewhere that they could not go. They had worked together as a team for the last 3½ years, and they had left everything and everybody they knew behind. To the disciples, it was apparent that there was still a lot of work to do. This gospel of the coming of the Kingdom of God had to be preached everywhere, including Rome and places even further away. This was no time for the leader to bail out. Besides, who was going to do all of that work?

It is here that we find our promise for today. Jesus told them, in the previous chapter, that they could not go with Him. This news was heart breaking. However, Jesus encourages them to not allow their hearts to be troubled. It was now time to believe, not just in God but in the power of His Son, Jesus. He told them there were many mansions in His Father's house, real mansions. He told them that He would prepare a place for them and that He would return to receive them unto Himself so that they would be where He was. Not only did they not need to fear His death, they did not need to fear their own. They would spend eternity with Christ.

That same promise is also for us that are born again. We will have eternal life with Jesus Christ. Because of that, we don't have to worry what will happen when we die. Will we stay in the grave until the rapture? Does our spirit immediately go to be with Christ? Is there a holding place somewhere? Will we be in heaven or will we be on earth?

You can have lots of fun proving or disproving the many theories there are associated with the afterlife, but there is one thing that is for sure. When it is all said and done, we will be with Him. That is the only thing that is important.

Affirmations

Jesus has prepared a place for me to be with Him forever. As a born again believer, I will have eternal life. I do not have to worry about dying. I rejoice and I am grateful for the promise that Jesus will come again and receive me and that where He is, I will be also. In Jesus Name, Amen.

Day 16 - Greater Works

Scripture Lesson: John 14:12

> Verily, verily, I say unto you, He that believeth on me, the works that I do shall he do also; and greater works than these shall he do; because I go unto my Father.

Meditation

It is hard to imagine doing greater works than Jesus Christ. He healed the sick, cast out demons and even raised the dead. He turned water into wine and fed many multitudes with very little food. He preached to thousands of people at a time and brought to them the good news about the Kingdom of God. How can we do greater works? Or better yet, why are we not doing greater works may be the more appropriate question.

Many of us read this scripture and look at it merely as words on a sheet of paper. Since we can't imagine doing even the works Jesus did, we disregard this statement and move on with our lives. Instead of this statement being a call to action for us, we see it simply as words that could never be meant to be taken literally. So not only do we not seek to do the "greater works" that Jesus describes, we have decided not even to do the works He did. Better yet, we will just sit back and let God do it all. Besides, we are not Jesus.

But we were made like Him. He is our brother, not our Father like we sometimes want to say. And as a big brother, He taught us how to walk in the power of God on earth. His disciples understood this to some degree because they were able to perform some of the same miracles He performed while He was alive and after He ascended.

Because of the advancements in the world, you can reach more people from your living room than Jesus could reach when He walked the earth. You have the ability to talk to more people via cell phones, text messages, Facebook and other social media in one day than Jesus could probably reach in a week. If you are in ministry, you can preach a sermon one time and it can be heard by millions on TV, radio and Internet at one time. And if someone needed to hear it again, there are archives. If you missed what Jesus had said the first time, you better hope that someone near you had a good memory. Think about it. The first Gospel published, which was the book of Mark, was written between 50 and 60 AD, at least 20 years after Jesus death. Before that time, it was only through the recollection of a few people or the word of mouth that someone could even hear the Gospel.

So, how do you do the greater works? One key is given in our verse, believe. The other key is in our promise for tomorrow which is in the very next verse: "And whatsoever ye shall ask in my name, that will I do, that the Father may be glorified in the Son" (John 14:13). You have to believe that you can do greater works. If you want to do it then just ask. Ask God to show you how to impact people with His good news.   Use the networks that you have established to spread the good news about God. Once you open yourself up to doing the works of God, trust me, plenty of opportunities to do "greater works" will present themselves.

Affirmations

I have been called to active duty. I believe that I can do what Jesus said I can do. I rejoice and I am grateful for the promise I can do the greater works that Jesus desires me to do. In Jesus' Name, Amen.

Day 17 - Ask Anything in My Name

Scripture Lesson: John 14:13-15

Whatsoever ye shall ask in my name, that will I do, that the Father may be glorified in the Son. If ye shall ask any thing in my name, I will do it. If ye love me, keep my commandments.

Meditation

Today we will continue to look at John 14-17 for promises that Jesus made to His people. It is one in the category that I call "blank check". Many teachers and preachers have placed limits on what Jesus could have meant when He said these words but the truth is there are no limits which Jesus speaks of. He purposely uses words such as "whatsoever" and "anything" to let us know exactly what He means. Whatsoever you shall ask in my name, that will I do. This sounds very similar to Mark 11:24; "What things soever ye desire, when ye pray, believe that ye receive them, and ye shall have them." Again we ask ourselves, how can Jesus make these types of promises?

The key is the power of our words and what we believe. It goes back to Mark 11:23 where Jesus explains the law of confession. For verily I say unto you, That whosoever shall say unto this mountain, Be thou removed, and be thou cast into the sea; and shall not doubt in his heart, but shall believe that those things which he saith shall come to pass; he shall have whatsoever he saith. Since many times we verbalize our prayers, it is only natural that what we pray, what we ask God, will fall into this category. Why would God give us so much power, especially when we could use it in the wrong way?

He has given us this power because He has given us dominion over the earth. That is a huge responsibility. With that huge responsibility, we need huge power. If we are going to operate in our promise from yesterday, which was to do "greater works", we need this type of power.

Now I know you are thinking...Jesus is not going to give us everything we ask or speak and really believe. What about things that are not good for us or things that are not His will? Well, I have a news flash, He has done it before. We have all confessed some things that we really wanted and got them. Some of them were not good things. We have used this law of confession in the world before we knew about the power of God. We spoke up on a lot of people, places and things that were not good for us, but they came anyway. We looked at those things as coming from the devil, and thereby gave him credit as a creator. Nowhere in the Word are we told that he has that type of power to create. The enemy just convinced us to use our words in a way that would kill, steal and destroy.

Since we have all of this power, what is keeping us from speaking up a bunch of stuff that does not edify God? Nothing. Many people who are not saved use these principles every day. Jesus does ask us a simple question: "What does it profit a man to gain the whole world but lose his soul"? You still have eternity to deal with. So how do we do this right? The answer is found in verse 15. If you love Jesus, keep His commandments. If you keep His commandments of loving God and then loving your neighbor, you won't use this power in the wrong way.

Affirmation

My words are powerful. Therefore, I will not use my words to hurt but to bring life to those around me. I believe that my prayers are answered. I rejoice and I am grateful for the promise that I can ask any thing in Jesus' name, and that He will do it. In Jesus' name, Amen.

Day 18 - Peace I Leave With You

Scripture Lesson: John 14:27-28

Peace I leave with you, my peace I give unto you: not as the world giveth, give I unto you. Let not your heart be troubled, neither let it be afraid. Ye have heard how I said unto you, I go away, and come again unto you. If ye loved me, ye would rejoice, because I said, I go unto the Father: for my Father is greater than I.

Meditation

The word "peace" used here is from the Greek word "ɛirēnē" which means security, safety, and prosperity. This is similar to the Hebrew word for peace "*shalowm*" which means completeness, safety, soundness (in body), welfare, health, prosperity, quiet, tranquility, and contentment. In this time of preparation, Jesus comforts his closest friends with this pronouncement of peace.

He further instructs them not to let their hearts be troubled. They were more than troubled. The disciples were scared. They did not understand what was going on. As we have said before, Jesus was again talking about leaving. Was this part of the plan? How could Jesus talk of leaving? There was so much left undone. It just did not make sense. They asked Jesus to explain it to them but His words did not make sense at this time. They would just have to trust Him.

This is where we find ourselves today. Sometimes things just don't make sense. Why are they acting this way? How could they release me from my job? How do they expect me to make it? And of course, one of the hardest questions, why did this person have to die? What do we do when we are bombarded with these questions, and the answers we get from God make no sense to us?

We must allow our hearts and minds to be engulfed in the peace that Jesus gives. We are to trust and depend on this peace to help us make it through. We must work hard to not allow our hearts to be troubled or afraid. Jesus goes one step further and tells them that if they loved Him, they would rejoice because He is going to be with His Father. What an awesome and profound state of mind Jesus desired for His disciples.

As we personally deal with the recent home going of three members in the body of Christ, who many of us knew, we must heed the words that Jesus spoke. Although our hearts are heavy, we must rejoice because they, just as Jesus, have gone home to be with their Father. Let our witness be the peace that Jesus has so graciously given us.

Affirmations

I choose to walk in the peace that Jesus has given to me. I will not let my heart be troubled or afraid. I know that in the peace Jesus gives there is completeness, safety, soundness, welfare, health, prosperity, tranquility, and contentment. I rejoice and I am grateful for the promise that Jesus has given me His peace. In Jesus' name, Amen.

Day 19 - Ask What You Will

Scripture Lesson: John 15:7

> *If ye abide in me, and my words abide in you, ye shall ask what ye will, and it shall be done unto you.*

Meditation

Today we will continue in what is believed to be one of Jesus' last discourse with his disciples. As we have seen in John chapter 14, Jesus tells us about a prepared place, the promise of the Holy Spirit and the greater works that He expects us to do. In chapter 15, Jesus explains how we will be able to accomplish all that is set before us. We must abide in Him and His words must abide in us.

Jesus begins this explanation with the illustration of a vine. He tells us that He is the vine and that His father is the gardener. As the gardener, God wants us to be fruitful. That which is not fruitful is removed. That which is fruitful is purged so that it will bear more fruit.

We then arrive at our promise for today. It is another "blank check" statement that appears to be on a totally different level than any that we have seen before. As Christians, we have always been taught that it is God's will that is important, not our will. And this, of course, is backed up with a number of scriptures, including Jesus crying out in the garden of Gethsemane, "not my will, but thy will be done". But here we see something that many of us have never seen before. Jesus says that you can ask what you will, and it shall be done.

There must be some mistake here. It was bad enough when He used words such as "whosoever" and "whatsoever". Now it appears that He is saying our will matters; that our desires count. What's the catch?

Well this time there does appear to be a catch. If we abide in Him and His Word abides in us, then we can stand on this promise. The more we abide in His word, the more our will and desires will line up with His. The more we abide in Jesus and in His Word, the more fruitful we will be. We are told in verse 8 that it is through our fruitfulness we glorify God.

So, today I challenge you. Do not allow the enemy of the Word to focus you on how the words Jesus spoke can't be true. If you allow the seed of doubt, concerning the words Jesus spoke, to be planted and nurtured in your mind, it will grow, and you will begin to doubt other words spoken by Jesus. Remember how the serpent tricked Eve regarding the words God spoke? If these promises seem just too far out there for you, do not be under condemnation. Ask God to give you wisdom and revelation. Focus your attention on abiding in Christ and His Word. Spend time in prayer, meditation, worship and study, not just reading God's Word.

Affirmations

I desire to be fruitful for the Lord. I will diligently seek God and abide in His Word. I rejoice and I am grateful for the promise that, as I abide in Jesus and His word, I can ask what I will, and it shall be done unto me. In Jesus' name, Amen.

Day 20 - Bring Forth Fruit

Scripture Lesson: John 15:16

> Ye have not chosen me, but I have chosen you, and ordained you, that ye should go and bring forth fruit, and that your fruit should remain: that whatsoever ye shall ask of the Father in my name, he may give it you.

Meditation

As Jesus continues talking with His disciples, He points out that He has chosen them. They did not choose Him as they think they did. What were they chosen to do? They were chosen to bear fruit, fruit that would remain. As you read further down in the chapter, Jesus explains He chose them out of the world. As a result, the world would hate them just as the world hated Him.

However, they were called to bring forth fruit. Even in an environment that did not like them and in an environment that wanted to see them fail, they were still called to bring forth fruit. What type of fruit were they to produce?

Many people connect this verse with the fruit of the Spirit that is listed in Galatians 5:22-23. It is very important that those 9 attributes listed in that scripture are apparent in our lives. When we walk in the Spirit our lives should exhibit love, joy, peace, longsuffering, gentleness, goodness, faith, meekness, and temperance. However, this is not the fruit that Jesus spoke of here since the disciples would not have been familiar with the fruit of the Spirit. Jesus explains the fruit that He is speaking of in the same verse. Let's read it again.

> *Ye have not chosen me, but I have chosen you, and ordained you, that ye should go and bring forth fruit, and that your fruit should remain: that whatsoever ye shall ask of the Father in my name, he may give it you.*

The fruit that Jesus speaks of here in verse 16 is the same as He spoke in verse 7. That fruit is the power of answered prayer. Whatsoever we ask of the Father in His name, He (the Father) may give it to us. This is repeated in verse 7 where He says "If ye abide in me, and my words abide in you, ye shall ask what ye will, and it shall be done unto you."

Our promise for today is the fruit that Jesus wants us to bear. God is not glorified by a bunch of empty words or unanswered prayers. He wants us to be fruitful and to experience manifestations to our prayers.

Affirmations

God has chosen me. He has chosen me to be fruitful. He has ordained me to be fruitful. I rejoice and I am grateful for the promise that whatsoever I ask of the Father in Jesus name, the Father will give it to me. In Jesus' Name, Amen.

Day 21 - He Will Guide You

Scripture Lesson: John 16:12-15

I have yet many things to say unto you, but ye cannot bear them now. Howbeit when he, the Spirit of truth, is come, he will guide you into all truth: for he shall not speak of himself; but whatsoever he shall hear, that shall he speak: and he will shew you things to come. He shall glorify me: for he shall receive of mine, and shall shew it unto you. All things that the Father hath are mine: therefore said I, that he shall take of mine, and shall shew it unto you

Meditation

Do you know that you have an inside connection to what is happening in heaven? It is better than any surveillance system that the CIA could ever dream of. You have access to conversations that are only happening in the spiritual realm. You are being shown things to come. You have the ability to know things that others could only dream of. How is all of this possible? Say good morning to the Holy Spirit.

As we continue listening to Jesus in one of His last major discourse with His disciples, we learn more about the job of the Holy Spirit. Jesus is sensitive to the hearts of His disciples. He makes mention in verse 6 that sorrow has filled their hearts. However, they have a big job to do. It will be up to this group of believers to spread the Gospel to the world.

He tells them that He still has many things to share with them but they cannot bear them now. Perhaps time was getting short. Jesus tells them that as they are getting closer to His time, He would not be speaking as much with them as He had in the past. Perhaps the disciples were too depressed at this time to really hear strong teaching and instruction. In any case, He had a plan. The Holy Spirit would have His work cut out for Him.

Not only would the Holy Spirit have to bring back to their remembrance things that Jesus had spoken to them in the past, the Holy Spirit would have to relay to them new teachings that Jesus had for them. Jesus tells them that the Spirit of Truth (which is just another name for the Holy Spirit) would guide them to all truth. However, He would not speak of himself. He would speak whatever it was that He heard and He would show them things to come. And make no mistake, Jesus makes it perfectly clear that the Holy Spirit is glorifying Him and showing them things that Jesus wants them to see.

The ministry of the Holy Spirit is vitally important today for believers. We are reminded in 1 Corinthians that we are the temple of the Holy Spirit. Do you realize how awesome this is? As we commune with the Holy Spirit, He tells us what He is hearing from Jesus. It is like having an inside reporter in heaven, telling us the latest news. We will not have to worry about knowing the will of God as long as we are listening to the Holy Spirit that is dwelling in us. Be sensitive to the leading of the Holy Spirit.

Affirmations

I will be sensitive to the voice of the Holy Spirit. I want to hear whatever it is that Jesus wants to tell me. I want to see whatever it is that Jesus wants to show me. I rejoice and I am grateful for the promise that whatsoever the Holy Spirit hears, that shall he speak: and the Holy Spirit will show me things to come. In Jesus' name, Amen.

Day 22 - Ask and You Shall Receive

Scripture Lesson: John 16:23-27

And in that day ye shall ask me nothing. Verily, verily, I say unto you, Whatsoever ye shall ask the Father in my name, he will give it you. Hitherto have ye asked nothing in my name: ask, and ye shall receive, that your joy may be full. These things have I spoken unto you in proverbs: but the time cometh, when I shall no more speak unto you in proverbs, but I shall shew you plainly of the Father. At that day ye shall ask in my name: and I say not unto you, that I will pray the Father for you: For the Father himself loveth you, because ye have loved me, and have believed that I came out from God.

Meditation

We come to the end of one of the final teachings that Jesus shared with His disciples.   Our promise for today has been repeated over 6 times in John chapters 14-16 and more than 10 times in the Gospels. Although our lessons may sound like a broken record, these scriptures are recorded separately. Whatsoever you ask the Father in my name, he will give it to you. He continues on to say ask and you shall receive so that your joy may be full. Why does Jesus have to keep repeating the same thing over and over?

It is obvious. This would be a challenging subject for God's children. But why? It doesn't make sense. If Jesus is going to take the time to tell the disciples this same thing over and over again, it must be important. Jesus did not spend this last good teaching session telling them about sin issues, living right or giving to the poor. He spent these last hours telling them to love each other. He told them about the greater works they would do, how to abide in Him, and the work of the Holy Spirit. But He also made them a promise; a promise that He repeated over 6 times in this one lesson. Ask the Father for what you want, and believe that you will receive it.

Here is the interesting thing. We still don't get it. After close to 2000 years, we still don't believe that you can ask God for what you want. We must make everything a struggle.   If you don't like what is happening in any area of your life, ask God to fix it. If your kids are acting up, ask God for what you want. If your boss does not treat you right, ask God to fix it. If you want your employees to have a better work ethic, ask God to fix it. Instead of complaining about what you don't have and what you don't want; ask God for what you desire.

Look at John 16:24. Read it over and over again until you get to the point that you believe what it says. Ask and you will receive so that your joy may be full. God wants you happy. He wants you full of joy. He does not want you beat up and broken down.

Perhaps, this is why we must come to God as a child. If you took a child to the store and told them that you would buy them whatever they wanted, they would not be in theological discussions about how this was too good to be true. They would race up and down the aisle getting what they want. Let's stop tell each other what we don't want and start asking God for what we do want. This is not prosperity teaching, "name it and claim it" theology or new age "ask the universe" stuff. This is what the Bible has instructed us to do.

Affirmations

I want to obey God's Word. Instead of complaining about what I don't want, I will ask God for what I do want. I rejoice and I am grateful for the promise that whatsoever I ask the Father in Jesus' name, He will give it to me. In Jesus' name, Amen.

Day 23 - Everlasting Life

Scripture Lesson: John 3:16

For God so loved the world, that he gave his only begotten Son, that whosoever believeth in him should not perish, but have everlasting life.

Meditation

Nicodemus was a Pharisee and one of the Jewish leaders of Jesus' day. As a Pharisee, he could not be seen speaking to Jesus in such an intimate conversation. Therefore he snuck to Jesus at night, when none of his colleagues were around. He doesn't ask Jesus anything, just gives Him a compliment of sorts. He had seen the miracles and was impressed. This man had to be a teacher from God.

Although Nicodemus was an educated man, he was entering a conversation that would prove to be well over his head. Jesus introduced an unfamiliar concept to him; the new birth. If you are not born again, Jesus told him, you cannot enter the Kingdom of God.

This idea did not sound inviting to Nicodemus. How could someone be born again? This was physically impossible. However, Jesus was not talking about a physical rebirth, it was a spiritual rebirth.

As Jesus explained this awesome concept to Nicodemus, He made a statement that would become the most popular verse in scripture. It is the central theme of the New Testament and our promise for today. "Because God loved the world, He gave His only begotten Son. Whosoever believes in Him will not perish but will have everlasting life."

What is everlasting life? Although we don't know what all it entails, we do know a few things. It does not speak of a never ending physical life as we know it. It speaks of an eternal life with Christ. We know that we will have new bodies. We know that there will be no more pain and no more tears. But most importantly, we will be with Christ.

So, when we lose loved ones who loved the Lord, we can find peace in knowing that their true life has not ended. Our earthly life is only a drop in the bucket when it comes to eternity. But what we do with this drop will determine where and how we will spend eternity.

Affirmations

God loves me. Because of this love, He gave His only Son Jesus. I believe Jesus is the Messiah. I rejoice and I am grateful for the promise that if I believe in Jesus, I will not perish, but I will have everlasting life. In Jesus' name, Amen.

Day 24 - I Will Give You Rest

Scripture Lesson: Matthew 11:28-30

Come unto me, all ye that labour and are heavy laden, and I will give you rest. Take my yoke upon you, and learn of me; for I am meek and lowly in heart: and ye shall find rest unto your souls. For my yoke is easy, and my burden is light.

Meditation

Our promise today is around a subject that many of us do not get enough of; rest. We are not super productive just because we are always doing something. Our schedules have gotten so busy that we hardly have time for those things that we say are a priority in our lives. We are always doing something. However, that something is not always producing what we need or desire in our lives. As a result, our relationships, our health and our spiritual walk suffers.

If you ask most people how they are doing, you will get some type of response that speaks to tiredness or fatigue. These same people will tell you that, for the most part, they are not particularly happy with their lives. So they are working hard but not seeing the accomplishments they desire. For these people (many of us would count ourselves in this group) Jesus provides an intriguing invitation. Come to me all you that labor and are heavy burdened and I will get you rest. Where do we sign up?

Then He tells us something that makes us think, "Ah, I knew it was too good to be true". He tells us to take His yoke upon us. Are you kidding me? My burdens are hard enough without taking someone else's yoke, especially the Savior of the world. "No thanks", we may say at first glance. "I'll just keep what I have."

But if we don't understand the yoking process and take time out of our busy schedules to learn of Him, we will miss the whole thing. A yoke is a harness or instrument placed upon two oxen, causing them to plow together. If one gets weak, he can be pulled by the other. Jesus tells us that His yoke is easy, and His burden is light. Since we know that it is not the work that is easy and light, it must be that Jesus is pulling most of the weight. That is not the Gospel of Jesus that most of us have heard preached. Many believe that Christianity is a hard and burdensome task that will keep you down. And as a result, we have turned many people away from the faith. Gandhi once said, "I like your Christ, I do not like your Christians. Your Christians are so unlike your Christ."

Our promise today is that Jesus will give us rest for our souls when we become yoked to Him. Remember, our soul is not our spirit. Our souls consist of our mind, intellect, and emotions. Could your mind use some rest? A rested mind learns how to work smarter, not harder. Learn of Jesus. Stop being weighed down by burdens you should not even be carrying. Find out what Jesus has already done for you by His grace.

Affirmations

I am yoked to Jesus. His strength carries my burdens and cares. I rejoice and I am grateful for the promise that I can find rest in Him. In Jesus' name, Amen.

Day 25 - Nothing Shall Be Impossible to You

Scripture Lesson: Matthew 17:20

And Jesus said unto them, Because of your unbelief: for verily I say unto you, If ye have faith as a grain of mustard seed, ye shall say unto this mountain, Remove hence to yonder place; and it shall remove; and nothing shall be impossible unto you.

Meditation

It appears that the disciples had a lot of opportunity to practice some of the things Jesus did before Jesus left. As we saw in Luke chapters 9 and 10, some of their exercises were a success. However, our lesson for today was not one of them.

As our story opens, a man brings his son to Jesus. The son is considered a lunatic and possessed by a demon. According to the father, he brought the boy to the disciples earlier, but they were not able to cure him. He was now bringing him to Jesus with the hope that maybe Jesus could do something.

Jesus' response addresses their unbelief. In both Matthew and Mark, Jesus speaks of their faithlessness. But whose faithlessness was he referring to? We find in our scripture for today that Jesus tells the disciples that they were not able to do this because of their unbelief. He then repeats what He has said several times before. If they could have just a little faith, they could speak to mountains, and they will move. As a result, nothing shall be impossible for them.

So, what was the mountain that needed to be removed here? Was it the demon? Not likely. They were familiar with casting out demons. In Luke 10:17, we find the disciples celebrating the fact that they had mastered "casting out demons 101". There was something here that was bigger than the demon that had to go.

It was the unbelief of the boy's father. We see in Mark 9:22-23 that Jesus had to address the unbelief of the father even before He dealt with the demon possessed boy. The father asks Jesus, "Is there anything you can do to help us?" Jesus reply was our promise a little while back, "Can you believe? All things are possible to him that believes." He then tells the disciples in Matthew's version of the story that if they have faith, nothing shall be impossible to them.

We see in Mark 6:5 that Jesus could do no mighty works one time while in Nazareth because of the unbelief of the people. Unbelief will hinder you from overcoming obstacles as well as not experiencing the full power and victory of God in your life.

The story goes on to include instructions about praying and fasting. Although we don't have time to deal with that portion of scripture right now, if you have a good study Bible, you will see there is a little controversy about whether this scripture was in the original manuscript. That is not our discussion today. It is important to fast and pray. However, if you fast and pray but don't deal with your unbelief, you will not see the results you desire.

Affirmations

I can do all things through Christ who strengthens me. I can overcome any obstacle, and I can take on any challenge. I will be honest about areas of unbelief and ask God to help me in those areas. I rejoice and I am grateful for the promise that nothing shall be impossible for me. In Jesus' name, Amen.

Day 26 - Your Father Will Forgive You

Scripture Lesson: Matthew 6:14-15

For if ye forgive men their trespasses, your heavenly Father will also forgive you: But if ye forgive not men their trespasses, neither will your Father forgive your trespasses.

Meditation

Let's be honest.   Forgiveness is one of those areas that many of us we tend to operate in a double standard.   When we do things wrong, we want the person to accept our apology quickly and forgive us.   However, if we are the ones that are wronged, we want the offending person to really understand what they did before they move to a status of forgiveness.   And don't let this be a repeat offense.   They would really be in trouble.

Jesus' teaching on forgiveness is probably one of the hardest lessons for most of us to comprehend.   Many of us may be able to forgive someone who made a mistake.   We may even be able to forgive someone that we believe did something on purpose.   However, Jesus' teaching on forgiveness is extreme.   In Matthew 18:22, we are to forgive the same person up to 490 times.   The world teaches us that this is just crazy.   Why would you allow someone to continue putting you in a position that requires you to constantly forgive them?   Is that wisdom?   What are the limits?

Now we want to put limits on Jesus.   When Jesus was telling us that all things are possible and that "whosoever" can ask "whatsoever", we were happy to find that there were no limits on Jesus.   Now that Jesus is talking forgiveness, we want to apply the brakes.

Our promise today tells us that God will forgive us if we forgive others.   It also states very clearly that God will not forgive us if we do not forgive others.   Jesus restates this in the Lord's Prayer and several other places.   Do you realize what this says?   Now we are not here to get into great theological debates but consider this.   The salvation provided to us by Jesus Christ includes God forgiving us for our sins.   If unforgiveness is going to cause God not to forgive us for our sins, then what does that do to our salvation?   Is there a place in the Kingdom of God for unforgiven Christians?   I do not know the answer, but I do know one thing.   I am not interested or willing to find out.   Our salvation in Jesus Christ is too precious to gamble with because of something that someone else did.   Unforgiveness is too expensive.

This is not easy.   It is very hard to forgive when you are angry and that is typically when the need for forgiveness arises.   You may feel that there is no way that you can forgive the person that hurt you because the offense is so bad.   But our big brother, Jesus, gives us the ultimate example.   Here is an opportunity to apply some of the other promises that we have learned. Earnestly pray (believe and receive) that God will give you a forgiving heart and then decide that you will walk in forgiveness, just like you walk in healing and prosperity.   Realize that nothing is impossible for you.   You can do all things.   You can forgive.   You will forgive.

Affirmations

I believe that I have what I say.   I will begin to walk in forgiveness.   I know that it is God's will for me to forgive.   I rejoice and I am grateful for the promise if I forgive men their trespasses, my heavenly Father will also forgive me.   In Jesus Name, Amen.

Day 27 - Keys of the Kingdom

Scripture Lesson: Matthew 16:19

> *And I will give unto thee the keys of the kingdom of heaven: and whatsoever thou shalt bind on earth shall be bound in heaven: and whatsoever thou shalt loose on earth shall be loosed in heaven.*

Meditation

Keys allow you access to places that are not accessible to the general public. When you give someone keys to your possessions, whether it is a house, car or an office, you give them authority to enter in. A key can also be something that gives an explanation or provides a solution, such as a key to a riddle or an answer key for a test. Here Jesus is giving His listeners both an explanation and authority regarding the kingdom of heaven.

The conversation that leads up to this promise began as a casual one. Jesus asked His disciples who did men think He was? There were several names that came up. Some thought He was John the Baptist, while other names were thrown around including Elijah, Jeremiah or one of the other prophets. Then Jesus made the question a little more personal. "Who do you think I am?" Peter stepped up to the plate and proclaimed that Jesus was the "Christ", the Messiah, the Son of the Living God. According to Jesus, Peter experienced what the church would be built on; revelation knowledge. Jesus explained that flesh and blood did not reveal this to Peter, but it was direct revelation from the Father. It was this revelation knowledge that Jesus would build His church on. Now many believe that Jesus was saying that He was building His church on Peter, but if you do a study on this verse you will see that He is using a play on words. The two words used here for rock, *petros* (Peter) means small stone while *petra* means foundational boulder. This revelation knowledge that Jesus is the Son of the Living God would be so powerful that the gates of hell would not be able to prevail against the church.

As with all things, knowledge is good. But if you lack wisdom, you will know information but not have the understanding on how to use it. I can know how the human brain works. I can also know how to cut things and how to sew things together. However, these bits of knowledge do not qualify me to perform brain surgery. The church would need more than just knowing that Jesus was the Messiah. The church would need a true revelation of what that meant and how to operate and walk in the authority of the Kingdom of God. The key to doing this is where we find our promise today.

This key has been repeated over and over in our promises; the power of our words. Whatsoever you bind on earth will be bound in heaven or in the spiritual realm. Likewise, whatever you loose on earth will be loosed in the spiritual realm. If you are speaking confusion, unbelief, lack and sickness, these are the things that you are setting loose in the spiritual realm. If you bind those things, they will not run rampant in your life. Use your keys to walk in the authority that God has given you.

Affirmations

I know that Jesus is the Son of the Living God. I also know that He has given me authority to walk in His power. I rejoice and I am grateful for the promise that whatever I bind on earth shall be bound in heaven: and whatever I loose on earth shall be loosed in heaven. I choose to bind strife, confusion, and bitterness. I choose to release faith, hope and, above all, love. In Jesus name, Amen.

Day 28 - No Condemnation

Scripture Lesson: John 5:24

> *Verily, verily, I say unto you, He that heareth my word, and believeth on him that sent me, hath everlasting life, and shall not come into condemnation; but is passed from death unto life.*

Meditation

Is there life after death? There are a ton of books that are filled with the opinions of great philosophers and theologians alike. Everyone wants to know what will happen when this assignment of living is over. Will we walk streets of gold or live in mansions? Will we see our dear departed love ones and friends? How will they look? Will we recognize anyone?

From what the Bible tells us, there is definitely life after death. However, it is not the life after death that we must concern ourselves with. It is the death after death. That's right. There is a death after this physical death that is described in Revelation 20:12-15 as the second death. However, the second death has no power over those that are a part of the first resurrection. Confused yet? If so, don't feel bad. That is probably how many of the people felt listening to Jesus as He told them about our promise for today.

In today's promise, Jesus speaks of passing from death unto life. Doesn't that seem strange? When people die, we say that they have "passed" meaning that they have passed from life unto death. But here Jesus tells His listeners that those that hear His Word and believe in His Father will have everlasting life and pass from death unto life. Jesus explains that there will be a resurrection for everyone in the grave, and all will be judged. According to John 5:9, those that have done good will have a resurrection of life, and those that have done evil will have a resurrection of damnation.

Hold on! Everyone has done evil before. Not only the Bible tell us that all have fallen short and sin, we know from our own experiences that we have all done evil in the past and there is 100% chance that we will do evil again. There are many judgments listed in the Bible, but this is probably the most important one. You fail this and your eternity may not be what you would want it to be. How can we avoid this resurrection of damnation?

The good thing is that Jesus is the judge and He has given us this promise. If we believe in Him, we will not come into condemnation. Whether or not you understand Bible eschatology, which is the study of end times, or the rapture or the first resurrection, your eternal salvation is secure if you trust in Jesus Christ. Although we may experience physical death, that death is only temporary. We will be raised and reign with Jesus if we believe in Him.

Affirmations

I thank God for Jesus Christ. It is through His sacrifice on the cross that I now have everlasting life.   I rejoice and I am grateful for the promise that if I hear His word, and believeth in His Father I will have everlasting life with no condemnation. In Jesus' name, Amen.

Day 29 - Justified By Your Words

Scripture Lesson: Matthew 12:35-37

A good man out of the good treasure of the heart bringeth forth good things: and an evil man out of the evil treasure bringeth forth evil things. But I say unto you, That every idle word that men shall speak, they shall give account thereof in the day of judgment. For by thy words thou shalt be justified, and by thy words thou shalt be condemned.

Meditation

If you look at all of the promises that Jesus specifically gave us, one thing is very clear. Jesus wanted us to understand the importance of our words. We have been told in a number of scriptures that we have what we say. There is power in our words. Although we say that we know this, our actions prove differently. We are quick to speak negative over situations, especially situations in our own lives. We will even use profanity and literally "curse" things that concern us. That's why it is called "cursing".

In our lesson today, Jesus puts forth one of His strongest arguments about the power of our words. Earlier in this chapter, Jesus tells His listeners about what has become to be known as the "unpardonable sin" or a sin that is unforgivable. What type of sin could we commit that Jesus or His Father would not forgive? Was it fighting, rape or murder? Not at all. It had nothing to do with what we did, who we slept with or who we stole from. It had to do with what we say about the Holy Spirit.

Then to top that off, we are told that we are going to have to give an account for every idle word in the Day of Judgment. Every time we "shoot our mouths off" we better aim at a target. Just like law enforcement must give an account for every bullet fired, we must give any account for every word we fire out.

Now here is the kicker. Jesus says we are justified and condemned by our words. Not by the words of others but by our own words. If you are constantly saying what you can't do or how bad things are, that is what you are going to get. It doesn't matter how many people pray and intercede on your behalf. If you are determined to curse yourself, no one, not even God, is going to step in to stop you. Meditate on this fact; you are justified or condemned by your words. You have more power than you think. We often blame God for things that He has clearly said are in our domain. We will pray for something, talk it down, and then say that it was God that did not want us to have it. This is clearly not what the Bible teaches.

Many Christians proclaim that they know the power of their words but then continue to say things that don't line up with the Word of God. But we get mad when we hear people, that are outside of the body of Christ, using the principles of Christ to accomplish what they wish to accomplish. All while we are not as effective as we could be, because we won't follow the rules. We have been taught the right way for years but without strong examples, we have fallen short. Let's commit to being an example that others can follow. Instead of saying, "Do as I say, not as I do" we can say, "Follow me as I follow Christ".

Affirmations

The words I speak are my law of good and they will produce the desired results because they are operated on by a power greater than I am. I rejoice and I am grateful for the promise that by my words I am justified. In Jesus' name, Amen.

Day 30 - My Words Shall Not Pass Away

Scripture Lesson: Luke 21:33
> *Heaven and earth shall pass away: but my words shall not pass away.*

Meditation

One of the things that really bothered Jesus' critics was the confidence in which He spoke. He did not speak as one of the scribes of that time. He spoke as someone with authority, as someone that knew what He was talking about. How could Jesus so confidently speak about things of the past, present and future? It was easy, because He knew His authority in all three time frames.

In our lesson today, the disciples ask Jesus about the end times. This conversation begins as a casual conversation about the temple. As they were admiring the magnificent temple, Jesus tells them that the temple would be destroyed. That was something hard for them to believe. It was so beautiful and strong. No one would dream of tearing it down. Surely Jesus was mistaken.

As they question Him further, Jesus tells them of the signs of the end of time. He explained that there would be pestilence, earthquakes and wars. He tells them not to be afraid when these things happen. As they were probably looking at Him like He was crazy, He tells them our promise for today. "Heaven and earth will pass away, but His words shall not pass away."

In times of uncertainty, we can find comfort in knowing that Jesus' words will not pass away. No matter how it looks, Jesus words will remain. There is no promise that Jesus has made that we can't stand on. Likewise, there is no warning that Jesus has given that we better not heed to. You can count on and depend on His Word.

Affirmations

I can depend on Jesus' words. I can stand on all of His promises. I must heed all of His warnings. I rejoice and I am grateful for the promise that heaven and earth will pass away: but His words shall not pass away. In Jesus' name, Amen.

Day 31 - I Am With You Always

Scripture Lesson: Matthew 28:18-20

And Jesus came and spake unto them, saying, All power is given unto me in heaven and in earth. Go ye therefore, and teach all nations, baptizing them in the name of the Father, and of the Son, and of the Holy Ghost: Teaching them to observe all things whatsoever I have commanded you: and, lo, I am with you always, even unto the end of the world.

Meditation

We will end our study of the promises of Jesus with what is known as the "Great Commission". For the disciples, it had been a long 3½ years. So much had happened and yet there was so much to be done. They had survived what was probably the most traumatic time of their lives, the crucifixion of Jesus Christ. Now they stood ready to take on this new challenge.

Although the crucifixion had been horrendous, Jesus was with them now. However, some among them still did not believe. At this point it didn't matter. Jesus' attention was towards the believers and those that would believe because of their work.

Jesus begins this commission with the proclamation that all power is given unto Him both in heaven and in earth. He had overcome every obstacle put in His way. He had defeated Satan. Now it was time to proclaim the Kingdom of God to all nations. He instructed them to go, teach and baptize all nations. What were they to teach? They were to teach people to observe all of the things Jesus had commanded.

Finally He ends with what is our promise for today. He promised that He would be with them always. They would not have to worry about being alone. They would not have to be overcome with fear and doubt. Jesus was with them.

This promise is extended to us today. Jesus promised that He would be with us, even until the end of the world. There is nothing that can separate us from His love. Regardless to our situations, we must know and have confidence that Jesus is with us always.

Affirmations

My brother Jesus has all power in heaven and on earth. He has commissioned me to go and teach others to observe all of the things He has commanded. I rejoice and I am grateful for the promise that He is with me always, even unto the end of the world. In Jesus' name, Amen.

Notes

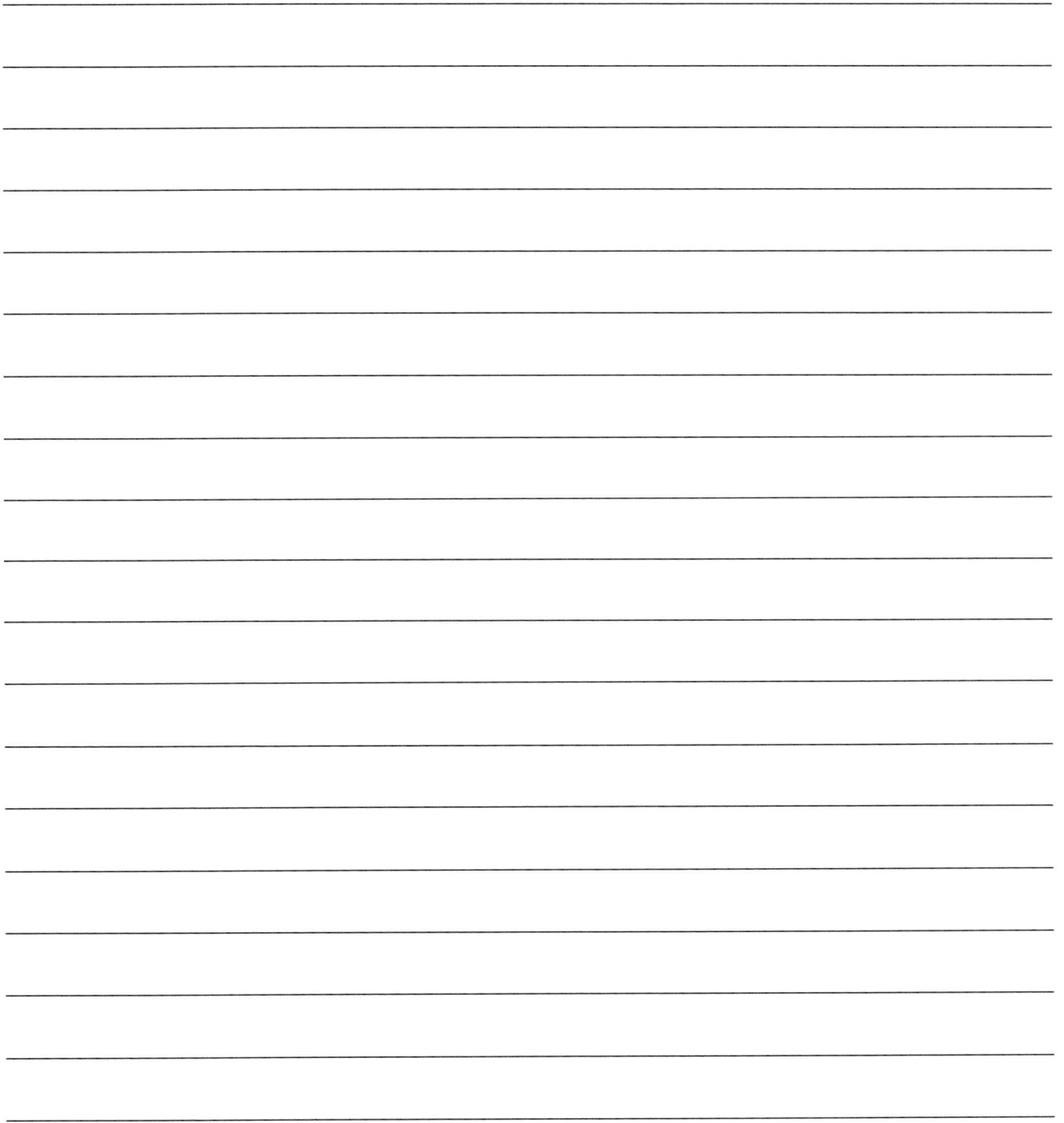

Other Books by Vanessa Collins

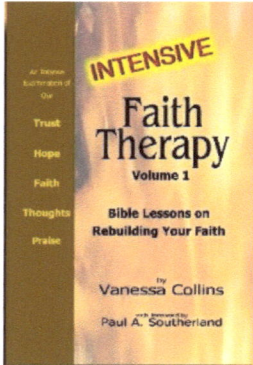

Intensive Faith Therapy
The Promises of God

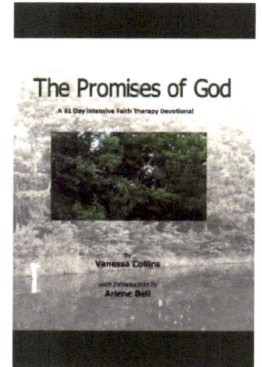

Looking for other materials to strengthen your faith?

Log on to www.IntensiveFaithTherapy.com

You can contact Vanessa Collins at Vanessa@intensivefaiththerapy.com or
Vancollins@aol.com

Look for us on Facebook
http://www.facebook.com/pages/Intensive-Faith-Therapy/111246621864

Follow us on Twitter
http://twitter.com/intensivefaith

Join our live class
http://pasenterprise.tv/IFT.html

www.ingramcontent.com/pod-product-compliance
Lightning Source LLC
Chambersburg PA
CBHW060812090426
42737CB00002B/39